HISTORIC CIVILIZATIONS

ANCIENT EGYPT

Anita Ganeri

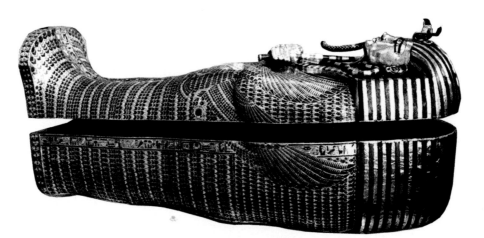

GARETH**STEVENS**

PUBLISHING

A World Almanac Education Group Company

How to Use This Book

Each topic in this book is clearly labeled and contains all these components:

Topic heading

Introduction to the topic

Subtopic 1 gives information about one aspect of the topic.

Words that are in the topic glossary are bolded the first time they appear on the page.

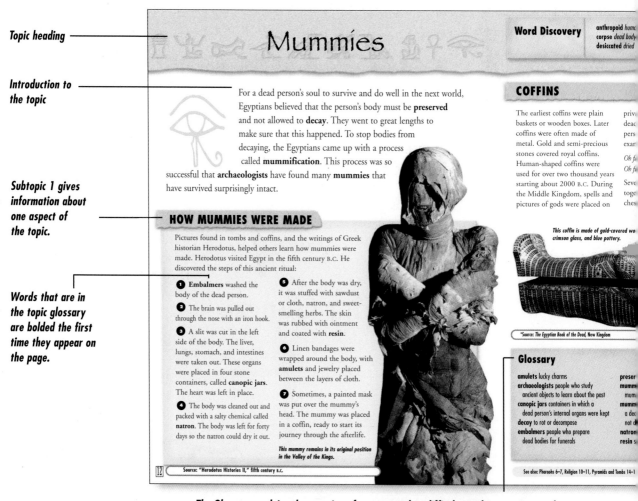

Mummies

Word Discovery
anthropoid *huma*
corpse *dead body*
desiccated *dried*

For a dead person's soul to survive and do well in the next world, Egyptians believed that the person's body must be **preserved** and not allowed to **decay**. They went to great lengths to make sure that this happened. To stop bodies from decaying, the Egyptians came up with a process called **mummification**. This process was so successful that **archaeologists** have found many **mummies** that have survived surprisingly intact.

HOW MUMMIES WERE MADE

Pictures found in tombs and coffins, and the writings of Greek historian Herodotus, helped others learn how mummies were made. Herodotus visited Egypt in the fifth century B.C. He discovered the steps of this ancient ritual:

❶ **Embalmers** washed the body of the dead person.

❷ The brain was pulled out through the nose with an iron hook.

❸ A slit was cut in the left side of the body. The liver, lungs, stomach, and intestines were taken out. These organs were placed in four stone containers, called **canopic jars**. The heart was left in place.

❹ The body was cleaned out and packed with a salty chemical called **natron**. The body was left for forty days so the natron could dry it out.

❺ After the body was dry, it was stuffed with sawdust or cloth, natron, and sweet-smelling herbs. The skin was rubbed with ointment and coated with **resin**.

❻ Linen bandages were wrapped around the body, with **amulets** and jewelry placed between the layers of cloth.

❼ Sometimes, a painted mask was put over the mummy's head. The mummy was placed in a coffin, ready to start its journey through the afterlife.

This mummy remains in its original position in the Valley of the Kings.

Source: "Herodotus Histories II," fifth century B.C.

COFFINS

The earliest coffins were plain baskets or wooden boxes. Later coffins were often made of metal. Gold and semi-precious stones covered royal coffins. Human-shaped coffins were used for over two thousand years starting about 2000 B.C. During the Middle Kingdom, spells and pictures of gods were placed on

priv
dead
pers
exan

*Oh fu
Oh fu*

Seve
toge
ches

This coffin is made of gold-covered wo crimson glass, and blue pottery.

Source: The Egyptian Book of the Dead, New Kingdom

Glossary

amulets lucky charms
archaeologists people who study ancient objects to learn about the past
canopic jars containers in which a dead person's internal organs were kept
decay to rot or decompose
embalmers people who prepare dead bodies for funerals

preser
mumm
mum
mumm
a dec
not d
natron
resin s

See also: Pharaohs 6–7, Religion 10–11, Pyramids and Tombs 14–1

The Glossary explains the meaning of any unusual or difficult words appearing on these two pages.

Please visit our web site at: **www.garethstevens.com**
For a free color catalog describing Gareth Stevens Publishing's list of high-quality books and multimedia programs, call 1-800-542-2595 (USA) or 1-800-387-3178 (Canada). Gareth Stevens Publishing's fax: (414) 332-3567.

Library of Congress Cataloging-in-Publication Data

Ganeri, Anita, 1961-
    Ancient Egypt / Anita Ganeri.
    p. cm. — (Historic civilizations)
    Includes index.
    ISBN 0-8368-4197-2 (lib. bdg.)
    1. Egypt—Civilization—To 332 B.C.—Juvenile literature. I. Title. II. Series.
DT61.G33   2004
932—dc22
                                        2004045305

This North American edition first published in 2005 by
Gareth Stevens Publishing
A World Almanac Education Group Company
330 West Olive Street, Suite 100
Milwaukee, Wisconsin 53212 USA

This U.S. edition copyright © 2005 by Gareth Stevens, Inc. Original edition copyright © 2004 ticktock Entertainment Ltd. First published in Great Britain in 2004 as *Your Ancient Egypt Homework Helper* by ticktock Media Ltd., Unit 2, Orchard Business Centre, North Farm Road, Tunbridge Wells, Kent TN23XF, UK.

The publishers wish to thank Anne Millard and Egan-Reid Ltd. for their research and consulting expertise in the making of this book.

Gareth Stevens editor: Barbara Kiely Miller
Gareth Stevens cover design: Steve Schraenkler

Printed in the United States of America

1 2 3 4 5 6 7 8 9 08 07 06 05 04

Contents

Subtopic 2 gives information about another aspect of the topic.

Discover other words that relate to the topic.

The Case Study is a closer look at a famous person, artifact, or building that relates to the topic.

excavated *dug out and removed or exposed*
fragrant *sweet-smelling*
priceless *very valuable*
purified *made clean or pure*
ornate *highly decorative*

CASE STUDY

o protect the
guide that
xt world. One
spells reads:

done no falsehood.
*ave not robbed.**

might be placed
large, stone
cophagus.

This death mask was found on the body of King Tutankhamun.

Each photo or illustration is described and discussed in the accompanying text.

A Famous Mummy

In 1922, British archaeologist Howard Carter made an astonishing discovery. In Egypt's Valley of the Kings, he found the tomb of Pharaoh Tutankhamun. The boy pharaoh was just nine years old when he came to the throne in about 1336 B.C. He was only nineteen or twenty years old when he died. Carter found an extraordinary treasure buried with the pharaoh. The most exciting find of all was described in Carter's diaries as:

*... a magnificent crystalline sandstone sarcophagus intact.**

The sarcophagus contained a set of three golden coffins. In the inner coffin was the mummified body of "King Tut" himself.

Source: Howard Carter, "The Discovery of the Tomb of Tutankhamun." Carter's diaries can be read online at: www.ashmol.ox.ac.uk/gri/4sea2sot.html

13

Captions clearly explain what is in the picture.

At the bottom of some sections, a reference bar tells where the information has come from.

ng time
ved by

ng and wrapping
ues so that it does

mmification
plant or tree

6–17

Other pages in the book that relate to what you have read in this topic are listed here.

A reference bar marked with an asterisk (*) gives the source of the quotations in the text.

The Land of Egypt

The **civilization** of ancient Egypt was one of the earliest and greatest in the world. It grew up on the banks of the Nile River as early as 3100 B.C. and lasted for several thousand years. The first people who settled in Egypt probably came from other parts of Africa to escape drought. Along the Nile, they began to build villages of mud huts, grow crops, and **domesticate** cattle.

FIRST DISCOVERIES

For about eighteen hundred years after the decline of its civilization, the secrets of ancient Egypt remained unknown. In 1822, however, a Frenchman named Jean François Champollion translated the Egyptian system of picture writing called hieroglyphics. Many ancient temples, **tombs**, **pyramids**, and cities were also explored at about the same time. These structures had been very well preserved by the dry, desert heat. The tombs were rich sources of information. Walls in the tombs were decorated with scenes of daily life and religious practices. People were often buried with their possessions, too. Items found in the tombs include jewelry, furniture, household objects, clothes, and food. Experts studied the tomb decorations and buried items. They were able to piece together a picture of life in ancient Egypt.

Many tomb paintings show the daily life of ancient Egyptians. This painting from the Sennedjem tomb in Thebes was made about 1250 B.C.

Source: Jean François Champollion, "Egyptian Diaries: A Voyage to the Mysteries of Egypt"
Notes and pictures from Champollion's trip to Egypt can be seen on the Internet at: www.touregypt.net/historicalessays/notes.htm

Word Discovery

artifacts *cultural objects*
Egyptology *study of ancient Egypt*
excavated *dug up*

linguist *someone who studies and speaks many languages*
mythology *set of beliefs*

New Kingdom *name of united Upper and Lower Kingdoms*
preserved *kept intact*

RULED BY KINGS

The villages of ancient Egypt grew into towns and cities. Eventually, two kingdoms were formed. The kingdoms were Upper Egypt in the Nile River Valley and Lower Egypt in the Nile **Delta**. King Menes ruled Upper Egypt. **Archaeologists** think that Menes united the two kingdoms into one in about 3100 B.C. To symbolize this unity, a double crown was worn by the rulers of Upper and Lower Egypt. The Greek historian Herodotus (b. 490 B.C.) wrote about Egyptian life and history. He had visited the country and talked to its priests. Herodotus wrote about the new capital that Menes built in Memphis:

> *When this Min (Menes), who first became King, had made into dry land the part which was dammed off, he founded in it that city which is now called Memphis ... Then secondly he established in the city the temple of **Hephaistes**, a great work and worthy of mention.**

*This statue of **Pharaoh** Ramses II shows him wearing the double crown of Up p er and Lower Egypt.*

*Source: "Herodotus Histories II," fifth century B.C. Read more at: www.touregypt.net/herodtusmenes.htm

Glossary

archaeologists people who study ancient objects to learn about the life of people in the past
civilization a culture and its people
delta area of soil sediment at the mouth of a river

domesticate to tame animals to live among and benefit people
Hephaistes Greek god of craftsmen, similar to the Egyptian god Ptah
pharaoh Egyptian ruler or king
pyramids triangular-shaped Egyptian tombs
tombs places where dead bodies are buried

CASE STUDY

The Nile River was vital for life to prosper in the deserts of Egypt.

The Nile River

More than 90 percent of Egypt is a hot, dry desert where little can grow. The ancient Egyptians called it "the Red Land." They lived on narrow strips of land on either side of the Nile River. Egypt's wealth was based on farming. Without the river, farmers would not have been successful. The importance of the Nile is revealed in an ancient poem called the "Hymn to the Nile":

Hail to thee, O Nile! Who manifests thyself over this land, and comes to give life to Egypt! Watering the orchards — created by Ra, to cause all the cattle to live, you give the earth to drink, inexhaustible one.*

See also: Language and Writing 8–9, Pharaohs 6–7, Religion 10–11, Farming 18–19

*Source: "Hymn to the Nile," c. 2000 B.C.

Pharaohs

Ancient Egypt was ruled by kings. Egyptians believed that kings were the god Horus in human form. The people thought a king was so holy that it was disrespectful to call him by his name. Instead, he was given the title of **pharaoh** which means "great house" or "palace." The pharaoh headed the government, kept law and order, led the army, and controlled trade and industry.

AKHENATEN & NEFERTITI

Akhenaten ruled ancient Egypt from about 1352–1336 B.C. His wife, Nefertiti, may have been his co-ruler for part of that time.

Letters sent to Akhenaten from kings and **officials** in different parts of the Middle East were discovered in 1887. Known as the Amarna letters, they tell what life was like during Akhenaten and Nefertiti's **reign**. One letter says that people in parts of the Egyptian **empire** felt neglected by the pharaoh:

And now your city weeps, and her tears are running, and there is no hope for us. For 20 years we have been sending to our lord, the King of Egypt, but there is not come to us a word, not one ...*

Another letter tells of a **plot** against Akhenaten.

You must know that Shipt-Ba'ad and Zimrida are conspiring. ... Now I have sent you Raphae-el. He will bring the Great Man intelligence concerning the matter.*

This painted limestone statue of King Akhenaten and Queen Nefertiti was found at Tell el-Amarna.

*Source: Amarna Letters, fourteenth century B.C. The Amarna letters can be read at: www.nefertiti.iwebland.com/amarnaletters.htm

Word Discovery

dynasty *a series of rulers from the same family or group*
monarch *royal ruler*

regal *royal or good enough for a king*
regent *someone who rules in*

place of the real king or queen
successor *next in line to the throne or position*

QUEENS OF THE NILE

Only a few rulers in ancient Egypt were women. The most remarkable of these was Queen Hatshepsut. She ruled from about 1490–1468 B.C. During her reign, Hatshepsut was addressed as "His Majesty." Sculptures often show her dressed as a man and wearing a **ceremonial** royal beard. She had a tomb in the Valley of the Kings and a beautiful funeral tomb at Deir el-Bahiri. Hatshepsut boasted that she had restored temples that were destroyed by earlier foreign invaders:

I have raised up what was dismembered even from the first time when the Asiatics were in the North Land.*

One of Egypt's most famous queens was Nefertiti. She may have co-ruled with her husband Akhenaten. Nefertiti was admired for her great beauty, and a sculpture of her head was found at Amarna. The last pharaoh to ever reign in Egypt was Cleopatra VII. She came from a Greek family.

Queen Hatshepsut was the most powerful female pharaoh. This statue comes from the side of Hatshepsut's temple in Deir el-Bahri.

Source: **Inscription on Hatshepsut's temple at Speos Artemidos, c. 1490 B.C.*

See also: Religion 10–11, Priests and Temples 16–17, Pyramids and Tombs 14–15, War and Weapons 24–25

CASE STUDY

Many statues of Pharaoh Ramses II still stand today, such as this one at Luxor.

Ramses the Great

Ramses II (or Ramses the Great) was one of Egypt's best-known kings. He ruled from about 1279–1213 B.C. During his long reign, he had more temples, statues, and monuments built to honor the gods than any other pharaoh. Ramses also led the Egyptian army in the Battle of Kadesh against the Hittites. The Hittites were the Egyptians' greatest enemy. Eventually, the two sides made peace. Descriptions of Ramses' army have been found carved onto walls:

... [covering] the mountains and the valleys; they were like grasshoppers in their multitudes.*

* Source: "The Poem of Pentaur," c. 1290 B.C.

Glossary

ceremonial part of or used during a ceremony
empire a group of lands ruled over by a single king or queen

inscription words or symbols written on a monument or other item
officials people who work for a government or in positions of authority

pharaoh ruler or king in ancient Egypt
plot a secret plan
reign the time that a king or queen rules over a country

Language and Writing

The ancient Egyptians were among the earliest people to write things down, beginning about 3500 B.C. They invented a **script** called **hieroglyphics** in which each hieroglyph, or picture, stood for an object, idea, or sound. The word hieroglyph was invented by the ancient Greeks and means "**sacred** carving." Writing was sacred to the Egyptians. They believed that Thoth, the god of wisdom, had given them the skill to write.

HOW HIEROGLYPHICS WORKED

There were over seven hundred hieroglyphic signs. Many of these signs were pictures of people, animals, and objects. Each sign could represent an object or idea or stand for the sound of one or more letters. Hieroglyphs were only written for consonants. In order to say a word, vowels had to be added. There were many different ways of writing hieroglyphs. They could be written from left to right, right to left, or top to bottom. If the signs for animals or people faced left, they were read from left to right. If the signs faced right, they were read from right to left. Hieroglyphs were used for important **inscriptions** on temples, tombs, and official records. The Egyptians used a much simpler and quicker script called **hieratic** for business, story-writing, and religious **documents**.

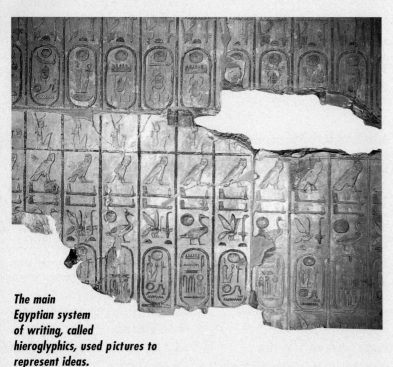

The main Egyptian system of writing, called hieroglyphics, used pictures to represent ideas.

Many examples of hieroglyphics have been discovered in tombs and temples. Some examples can be seen on the Internet at: www.thebritishmuseum.ac.uk

Word Discovery

breakthrough *great success* **communication** *the exchange of information through a common*	*system of symbols or signs* **decipher** *to decode* **palette** *a box containing*	*inks and brushes* **represent** *stand for* **scholar** *expert*

SCRIBES

Hieroglyphs were very complicated. Professional writers, called **scribes**, had to be trained at special schools. The training started when a boy was about nine years old and lasted for seven to twelve years. After students were good enough, they were allowed to write on **papyrus** scrolls. They used reed pens dipped in red or black ink. Good scribes might work in a temple, the law court, or the government. They might travel with the army to write battle reports. Students were given lots of advice:

Apply yourself to this noble profession. You will be advanced by your superiors. Love writing, shun dancing, do not long for the marsh thicket. By day write with your fingers; recite by night. Befriend the scroll ... it pleases more than wine. *

Scribes were usually shown sitting cross-legged and holding their writing materials. This statue of a scribe is from a tomb at Saqqara.

*Source: "Papyrus Lansing," Late New Kingdom.

Glossary

demotic Egyptian shorthand script
documents official papers
hieratic a simple style of Egyptian writing used in everyday life
hieroglyphics ancient Egyptian style of writing using pictures
inscriptions words written on paper, stone, or metal
papyrus a paperlike material made from reeds and written on
sacred holy
scribes professional writers
script the signs or letters used to write a language down

See also: The Land of Egypt 4–5, Work and Play 20–21, War and Weapons 24–25, Families 28–29

CASE STUDY

The 1799 discovery of the Rosetta Stone led to the translation of the ancient Egyptian language.

The Rosetta Stone

The Roman empire conquered ancient Egypt more than two thousand years ago. Afterward, the art of reading and writing hieroglyphs gradually ended. Then, in 1799, a French soldier in Napoleon Bonaparte's army made a thrilling discovery in Rosetta, Egypt. He found a large, stone slab covered with ancient writing. On the stone, the same text was written in three different scripts — hieroglyphic, **demotic**, and Greek. A Frenchman named Jean François Champollion knew the Greek language. He compared the other two scripts to the Greek. By doing this, he was able to finally crack the code and solve the mystery of how to read and understand hieroglyphs.

Source: Jean François Champollion, "Egyptian Diaries: A Voyage to the Mysteries of Egypt" www.touregypt.net/historicalessays/notes.htm

Religion

The ancient Egyptians worshiped dozens of gods and goddesses. Egyptians believed these **deities** ruled the natural world and controlled all aspects of daily life. Some gods and goddesses were worshiped everywhere in Egypt. Others were special only to certain cities or towns.

KING OF THE GODS

One of the most important gods in Egyptian religion was Ra, the sun-god. He had many different forms and names. He is often shown in paintings as a man with a hawk's head. A sun disk surrounded by a cobra is shown above his head.

The ancient Egyptians believed that Ra created the world and everything in it. According to Egyptian **mythology**, he set sail across the heavens every morning in a boat. At night, Ra sailed through the **underworld**. He brought light to the dead and left the world in darkness. He rose again into the sky every morning. Later, Ra was merged with the god Amun. He became Amun-Ra, king of the gods. Ra's powers are praised in the Egyptian *Book of the Dead*:

*The gods rejoice when they see Ra crowned upon his throne, and when his beams flood the world with light ... May Ra give glory, and power, and truth-speaking ... Hail you gods of the house of the soul, who ... give celestial food to the dead.**

This statue is of Horus, the falcon-headed god of the sky. He was the guardian of the king and the son of Isis and Osiris.

*Source: "A Hymn of Praise to Ra when he rises in the eastern part of Heaven" from the *Egyptian Book of the Dead*, New Kingdom

Word Discovery

inscription words carved on a monument or other surface
pilgrims people who travel to shrine or holy place
reincarnation being born again in a new body or form
sacrifice offer something of value to a god
spiritual religious

LIFE AFTER DEATH

The Egyptians believed in a life after death, which they called the next world. Before a person's **soul** could enter the next world, it had to go through a series of trials in the underworld. If their soul passed these tests, it entered the **Judgment** Hall of Osiris. He was ruler of the dead. Once there, the soul had to recite the "Negative Confession" with the following promises:

I have not committed sin ... I have not committed robbery with violence ... I have not stolen ... I have not uttered curses ... I have not uttered lies ... I have not been angry without just cause ... I have not eaten the heart ... I have not slandered any man ... I have terrorized none. *

Dead souls were tested in the Judgment Hall of Osiris. The tests told if a person had led a good or a bad life.

There were many Egyptian gods and goddesses. Some of the more common ones were:

Isis	mother goddess
Maat	goddess of truth and justice
Osiris	god of the underworld
Rasun	god
Thoth	moon god
Hathor	goddess of love
Ptah	god of craftsmen

*Source: "The Negative Confession," from the *Egyptian Book of the Dead*, New Kingdom

CASE STUDY

Sacred Cats

The Egyptians thought some animals, such as cats, bulls, and the ibis bird, were **sacred**. They believed the animals were the earthly forms of gods. Anyone who deliberately killed a cat could be sentenced to death. When cats died, they were **mummified** and some were put in cat-shaped coffins. These coffins were sold to temple visitors who could bury them in the temple **cemetery** as an offering to the cat goddess, Bastest. Another important cat protected the sun-god, Ra. In Thebes, a tomb inscription reads:

*Thou art the Great Cat, the avenger of the gods, and the judge of words, and the president of the **sovereign** chiefs and the governor of the holy Circle; thou art indeed ... the Great Cat.* *

Many cat statues have been found in Egyptian tombs. This statue from Saqqara was made about 600 B.C.

*Source: Inscription on the Royal Tombs at Thebes, New Kingdom

Glossary

cemetery burial ground
deities gods or goddesses
judgment decision or opinion
mummified embalmed, dried, and wrapped in bandages as a mummy
mythology stories and legends about gods and goddesses
sacred holy
soul the spirit of a person that lives on after death
sovereign a supreme ruler
underworld the home for the dead in Egyptian mythology

See also: Pharaohs 6–7, Mummies 12–13, Pyramids and Tombs 14–15, Priests and Temples 16–17

Mummies

For a dead person's soul to survive and do well in the next world, Egyptians believed that the person's body must be **preserved** and not allowed to **decay**. They went to great lengths to make sure that this happened. To stop bodies from decaying, the Egyptians came up with a process called **mummification**. This process was so successful that **archaeologists** have found many **mummies** that have survived surprisingly intact.

HOW MUMMIES WERE MADE

Pictures found in tombs and coffins, and the writings of Greek historian Herodotus, helped others learn how mummies were made. Herodotus visited Egypt in the fifth century B.C. He discovered the steps of this ancient ritual:

1 **Embalmers** washed the body of the dead person.

2 The brain was pulled out through the nose with an iron hook.

3 A slit was cut in the left side of the body. The liver, lungs, stomach, and intestines were taken out. These organs were placed in four stone containers, called **canopic jars**. The heart was left in place.

4 The body was cleaned out and packed with a salty chemical called **natron**. The body was left for forty days so the natron could dry it out.

5 After the body was dry, it was stuffed with sawdust or cloth, natron, and sweet-smelling herbs. The skin was rubbed with ointment and coated with **resin**.

6 Linen bandages were wrapped around the body, with **amulets** and jewelry placed between the layers of cloth.

7 Sometimes, a painted mask was put over the mummy's head. The mummy was placed in a coffin, ready to start its journey through the afterlife.

This mummy remains in its original position in the Valley of the Kings.

Source: "Herodotus Histories II," fifth century B.C.

Word Discovery

anthropoid *human-shaped*
corpse *dead body*
desiccated *dried up*

excavated *dug out and removed or exposed*
fragrant *sweet-smelling*

priceless *very valuable*
purified *made clean or pure*
ornate *highly decorative*

COFFINS

The earliest coffins were plain baskets or wooden boxes. Later coffins were often made of metal. Gold and semi-precious stones covered royal coffins. Human-shaped coffins were used for over two thousand years starting about 2000 B.C. During the Middle Kingdom, spells and pictures of gods were placed on private coffins to protect the dead person and guide that person to the next world. One example of such spells reads:

Oh far strider, I have done no falsehood. Oh fire-embracer, I have not robbed.

Several coffins might be placed together inside a large, stone chest called a sarcophagus.

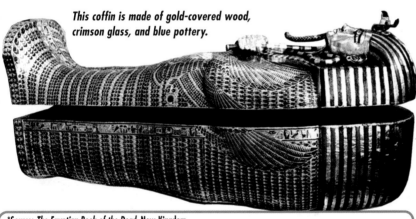

This coffin is made of gold-covered wood, crimson glass, and blue pottery.

Source: The Egyptian Book of the Dead, New Kingdom

CASE STUDY

This death mask was found on the body of King Tutankhamun.

A Famous Mummy

In 1922, British archaeologist Howard Carter made an astonishing discovery. In Egypt's Valley of the Kings, he found the tomb of Pharaoh Tutankhamun. The boy pharaoh was just nine years old when he came to the throne in about 1336 B.C. He was only nineteen or twenty years old when he died. Carter found an extraordinary treasure buried with the pharaoh. The most exciting find of all was described in Carter's diaries as:

... a magnificent crystalline sandstone sarcophagus intact.

The sarcophagus contained a set of three golden coffins. In the inner coffin was the mummified body of "King Tut" himself.

Source: Howard Carter, "The Discovery of the Tomb of Tutankhamun." Carter's diaries can be read online at: www.ashmol.ox.ac.uk/gri/4sea2not.html

Glossary

amulets lucky charms
archaeologists people who study ancient objects to learn about the past
canopic jars containers in which a dead person's internal organs were kept
decay to rot or decompose
embalmers people who prepare dead bodies for funerals

preserved kept for a long time
mummies bodies preserved by mummification
mummification preserving and wrapping a dead body in bandages so that it does not decay
natron salt used for mummification
resin sticky gum from a plant or tree

See also: Pharaohs 6–7, Religion 10–11, Pyramids and Tombs 14–15, Priests and Temples 16–17

Pyramids and Tombs

To make sure that their bodies were preserved forever, the Egyptian pharaohs had huge **tombs** built for themselves. They hoped that their bodies and the precious things they were taking with them into the next world would be safe in the tombs. The first pyramid was built as a tomb for King Zoser in about 2680 B.C. It had stepped sides that represented a giant stairway that would allow the king's soul to climb to heaven. Later, pyramids were built with straight sides to **symbolize** the sun's rays.

HOW TO BUILD A PYRAMID

Historians think that the Egyptians built the pyramids this way:

1 Teams of builders used wooden sleds to drag cut stone blocks into position.

2 The blocks were pulled up a ramp made of brick and mud.

Much of what is known about building the pyramids came from **excavations**. The Greek historian and writer Herodotus described the tomb builders at the Great Pyramid of Giza:

The stones were quarried in the Arabian mountains and dragged to the Nile. They were carried across the river in boats and then dragged up the slope to the site of the pyramid ... They worked in gangs of 100,000 men, each gang for three months. The pyramid itself was twenty years in the making. *

Despite Herodotus' claim, scholars today believe that only twenty thousand men were involved in the building of this pyramid.

*Source: "Herodotus Histories II," fifth century B.C.

Word Discovery

adorned *decorated*
architect *person who designs buildings*

constructed *built*
implements *tools*
limestone *a soft stone used*

for building
looted *robbed*
majestic *grand*

THE VALLEY OF THE KINGS

Later pharaohs chose to be buried in tombs cut deep into the cliff face in the Valley of the Kings. This remote valley was on the edge of the desert to the west of the city of Thebes. Inside, the tombs were decorated with scenes from the next world. Non-royal tombs were decorated with scenes of daily life. Both royal and non-royal tombs were filled with treasure, and they became a target for robbers. The problem of **tomb robbers** comes to life in the popular story *Ali Baba and the Forty Thieves:*

Many pharaohs were buried in Thebes' Valley of the Kings.

... when the chamber was finished, the king stored his money in it ... but when upon his opening the chamber a second and a third time the money was each time seen to be diminished, for the thieves did not slacken in their assaults upon it, ... having ordered traps to be made he set these round about the vessels in which the money was; ... Now when it became day, the king entered into the chamber and was very greatly amazed, seeing the body of the thief held in the trap without his head ...

*Source: "Herodotus Histories II," fifth century B.C.
The entire tale of Ali Baba can be read on the Internet at: www.nefertiti.iwebland.com/herodotus/rhampsinitos.htm

Glossary

excavations holes formed and things exposed by digging
sarcophagus a stone chest in which bodies are buried
symbolize to stand for something; have a special meaning

tombs places where bodies of dead people are buried
tomb robbers people who broke into the pyramids and royal tombs and stole the treasures inside

CASE STUDY

The Great Pyramid

The Great Pyramid of Giza is the largest pyramid and one of the seven wonders of the ancient world. According to the writings of Manetho and Herodotus, the pyramid was built for King Khufu about 4,500 years ago. Originally, it stood 481 feet (147 meters) tall. The pyramid contains about 2.3 million blocks of limestone, each weighing about 2.8 million tons (2.5 tonnes). The king's mummified body was buried in a stone **sarcophagus** in the King's Burial Chamber, deep inside the pyramid. In the Middle Kingdom, pharaohs had false passages and secret entrances added to tombs. They wanted to stop robbers who might try to steal treasures buried with the king. Even with these changes, treasures were stolen.

The Great Pyramid of Giza was the tallest building in the world for nearly 4,500 years.

Explore the Great Pyramid on the Internet at: www.pbs.org/wgbh/nova/pyramid/explore/khufu.html

See also: Pharaohs 6–7, Religion 10–11, Mummies 12–13, Priests and Temples 16–17, Trade and Transportation 22–23

Priests and Temples

Egyptian temples were used to honor one particular god or goddess. The people believed that temples were the gods' homes on Earth. Only priests and priestesses were allowed to go inside the temples to worship. Ordinary Egyptians could say prayers and leave offerings for the gods only at the temple entrance or in the courtyard. As chief priest, the pharaoh could not visit every temple in Egypt. Instead, he appointed priests to perform the ceremonies for him.

TEMPLES

According to archaeological remains and art, a typical Egyptian temple followed this plan:

• A temple was surrounded by an outer wall (A). Inside was a courtyard. A pylon, or temple gateway (B), then led to the temple enclosure.
• The main part of the temple had a pylon that often had on each side two needle-shaped monuments, called obelisks. These monuments were dedicated to the sun-god.
• Inside the temple were one or more spacious courtyards (C).
• Next came the hall of columns (D), which would have been decorated with many **reliefs** and columns.
• At the back was the **sanctuary** (E), which was the most holy part of the temple. The sanctuary contained the **shrine** in which the statue of the temple god or goddess was kept.

Egyptians celebrated many annual festivals in honor of the gods and goddesses. On these special days, people were allowed inside the temples to celebrate. One example is the "Beautiful Festival of the Valley." During this festival, people dressed in their best clothes and visited the tombs of loved ones. The calendar dates of many Egyptian festivals were found inscribed on temple walls.

Source: Temple of Ramses III at Medinet Habu, c. 1180 B.C.

Word Discovery

ceremonies *formal occasions*   *in an orderly line*   *god or gods*
pious *very religious*   **purify** *make clean or pure*   **worshiping** *honoring gods*
procession *parade or moving*   **religious** *believing in a*

PRIESTS

Each temple had priests who performed religious **rituals**. They also supervised the temple industries, which may have included baking, brewing beer, and tending the temple's lands. As payment, priests received a share of the food offered daily at the temple. One important duty of the priests was preparing dead bodies for burial:

> *I decked the body of the lord of Abydos with ... every costly stone, among the ornaments of the limbs of a god. I dressed the god in his regalia by virtue of my office as master of secret things, and of my duty as priest.**

Priests could become very wealthy. The ancient writer Homer described the rich priesthood at Thebes:

> *The heaps of precious* **ingots** *gleam, the hundred-gated Thebes.**

This statue of a priest named Hetepdief is from about 2650 B.C.

*Sources: The Ikhernofret Stela c. 1860 B.C. and The Iliad, Book 9, c. 700 B.C.

CASE STUDY

Temple of Luxor

The Temple of Luxor was built by Pharaoh Amenhotep III. Located in Thebes close to the Nile River, it was dedicated to the god Amun-Ra. Later additions to the temple were built by other pharaohs, such as Ramses II. The temple is 850 feet long (259 m) and 213 feet (65 m) wide in the front. In ancient times, a 2-mile (3-kilometer) avenue of **sphinxes** stood between it and the Temple of Karnak. During Luxor's great celebration, the Festival of Opet, a sacred statue of Amun was taken in a procession from Karnak to Luxor over land and by river.

Two long lines of sphinxes once stretched all the way from Luxor to Karnak. Some of these sphinxes are still standing.

Glossary

ingots blocks of metal, such as gold
reliefs sculptures with carved images projecting from a flat surface
rituals actions performed during a religious ceremony
sanctuary the holiest part of a temple
shrine part of a temple with a statue of a god, goddess, or saint
sphinxes sculptures with lion's body and man's, hawk's, or ram's head

See also: Pharaohs 6–7, Religion 10–11, Pyramids and Tombs 14–15, Work and Play 20–21

Farming

Many ancient Egyptians worked as farmers along the Nile River. Most people did not own their own land. Instead, they farmed land that was a part of large estates that belonged to wealthy government officials or temples. Farmers kept part of their crops for themselves but had to pay taxes to the landowner and to the pharaoh each year. They were punished if they failed to do this. The Egyptian farming year was divided into three seasons.

GROWING AND HARVESTING

*This wooden model of a granary with figures is from Thebes, Egypt, **Middle Kingdom**, about 2000–1800 B.C.*

Scenes and small models found in tombs across Egypt help explain the system of farming in ancient times.

The growing season started in November when the farmers plowed the land and sowed the seeds. Harvesting began in March and was done by hand, using wooden and flint **sickles**. The harvested grain was taken to the **threshing** floor where cattle trampled it to separate the grain from the stalks. Next, the grain and **husks** were separated, and the grain was kept in storehouses called **granaries** until it was needed. Models of these granaries suggest that bread was made there as well. Farmers worked very hard, as described in this account written during the late-New Kingdom by the scribe Nebmare-nakht:

By day he cuts his farming tools; by night he twists rope. Even his midday hour he spends on farm labor.

Word Discovery

agriculture *farming*
deposited *left*
livestock *farm animals*

plots *small pieces of land*
productive *producing in big amounts*

subsided *went down*
tending *looking after*

CROPS AND ANIMALS

Wheat and barley were important crops for Egyptian farmers.

The type of crops planted in ancient Egypt have been discovered through written texts and the actual dried remains of plants. The most common crops seem to have been barley and wheat. Wheat was used to make bread and barley to make beer. Egyptians grew vegetables such as onions, garlic, lentils, beans, and lettuce. They grew grapes for making wine, too. Archaeologists have also found the bones of cattle, pigs, sheep, and goats that date from this time. Egypt's harsh climate had a huge effect on a farmer's **yield**. An ancient text has been found in which one angry farmer faces this problem:

Now, what do you mean by having Sihathor coming to me with old, dried-out, northern barley from Memphis, instead of giving me ten sacks of good, new barley?*

*Source: Hekanakhte's letters, c. 2000 B.C.

Glossary

fertile good for farming (land)
granaries buildings for storing grain
husks the dry outer covering of fruits and seeds
Middle Kingdom the name given to united Egypt between 2055 and 1650 B.C.
nilometers steps with scales carved in the sides that measured the height of the Nile River
sickles sharp, hook-shaped tools for cutting grain
threshing beating the grain in order to separate the grain from the stalks
yield amount of crops produced

CASE STUDY

Nilometers were built to measure the Nile River during flood season.

Floods

The flood season started each July. The Nile River overflowed and flooded its banks, spreading **fertile**, black soil on the fields. Farm work came to a halt while the fields were under water. During this time of year, many farmers were called upon to build royal tombs. The writer Herodotus recorded the importance of the Nile's annual floods:

It is certain that now they gather in fruit from the earth with less labor than any other men ... the river has come up of itself and watered their fields.*

See also: The Land of Egypt 4–5, Work and Play 20–21, Trade and Transportation 22–23, At Home 26–27

*Source: "Herodotus Histories II," fifth century B.C.

Work and Play

Most Egyptians worked as farmers and builders. If a man was well educated, however, he might get a job as a **scribe**, priest, or government official. Skilled craftsmen were always in demand for making essential everyday items, such as pots, baskets, and sandals. Women were expected to tend to **domestic** duties. In their spare time, Egyptians celebrated religious festivals with music and dancing. Wrestling and hunting were favorite sports.

ROYAL TOMB BUILDERS

The artists and craftsmen who worked on the royal tombs in the Valley of the Kings lived in a specially built village named Deir el-Medina.

These **artisans** left written records that describe the way in which they worked. About sixty workmen were divided into two groups, each led by a **foreman**. The people who decorated the inside walls with paintings and hieroglyphs were just as important as those who constructed the tombs. Many documents survive that reveal just how skilled these artists were:

I know how to render the posture of a man's statue, the step of a woman's statue, the wing strength of a dozen birds, the bearing of him who strikes a prisoner, the look an eye casts on someone else and also make fearful the face of the sacrificial victim, the arm of him who hits the hippopotamus, the stance of the runner. *

This wall painting from Deir el-Medina shows builders making mud bricks for an Egyptian's tomb.

*Source: Mortuary inscription of Irtysen, New Kingdom

Word Discovery

appreciated *enjoyed*
entertainment *fun event or activity*

festivities *celebrations*
income *money earned*
leisure *free time*

manual *done by hand*
pastime *hobby*
supervised *watched over*

GAMES

Senet was a popular board game that was enjoyed even by the pharaohs.

Children in ancient Egypt loved playing with toys just as children do today. Many toys have been found in the graves of Egyptian children. These toys included tops, wooden animals on wheels, colorful clay balls filled with beads or seeds that rattled when thrown, and dolls made from wood. Board games were also popular. In a game called senet, players had to try to overcome various dangers to reach the Kingdom of **Osiris**. Four senet boards were found in Tutankhamun's tomb, showing that even the pharaohs enjoyed this game. One of the earliest games played in Egypt was called "the game of snake" because the board was shaped like a coiled serpent. The first player to reach the snake's head in the center was the winner.

CASE STUDY

MUSIC

Wealthy Egyptians liked to entertain by holding large **banquets** that included music and dancing. They hired **professional** musicians and dancers who performed while the guests ate. Paintings found inside tombs show that Egyptian musicians played harps, **lyres**, cymbals, and flutes. Tomb inscriptions describe the beauty of some instruments:

My majesty made a splendid harp wrought with silver, gold, lapis lazuli, malachite, and every splendid costly stone.*

Many musical instruments have been preserved in tombs. The words to songs were often written on tomb and temple walls.

Harp music was an important part of Egyptian celebrations.

Glossary

artisans skilled workers
banquets sumptuous meals or parties
domestic relating to the home
foreman someone in charge of the work of others

lyres ancient musical instruments with strings
Osiris Egyptian god of the dead
scribe professional writer
professional doing something as a paid job

*Source: Coronation inscription of Thutmosis III, c. 1500 B.C.

Trade and Transportation

The Nile River was the main **transportation** route through ancient Egypt. Most people lived near the river, and it was the best way to make long journeys north and south through the country. Trade with the neighboring land of Nubia was so important that the Egyptians cut a special canal from the Nile to Nubia for quicker journeys. They also sailed on the Mediterranean Sea to trade with the other countries around it.

BUYING AND SELLING

The ancient Egyptians did not use money. Instead, they traded one set of goods for another set of goods that had the same value. This system of trading was called **bartering**.

Gold rings are being weighed to see how many deben they are worth in this painting from the tomb of Panekhmen.

Later, a new system of trading was introduced. The value of goods was decided by how many **debens,** or copper weights, an item was worth. One deben was divided into ten smaller weights, called kites. According to ancient texts, traders had to obey strict rules or they would face the anger of the gods:

Do not move the scales, do not change the weights. He loathes (Re) him who defrauds. *

Egypt was in a good location for trading with other countries in Africa and around the Mediterranean Sea. The exotic goods that were traded include gold, ivory, **ebony** and other valuable woods, leopard skins, and live animals.

*Source: "The Teachings of Amenemope," late New Kingdom

Word Discovery

cargo *goods carried by ship or vehicle*

economy *a country's wealth*

exports *goods sold to other countries*

imports *goods bought from*

other countries

merchants *people who trade goods for a living*

SHIPS AND BOATS

Boats were the quickest and easiest way to travel in Egypt and were the main form of transportation. The Egyptians were skilled shipbuilders. Their earliest boats were made from bundles of reeds tied together. These boats were used for short hunting or fishing trips. Later, larger boats were made of wood with both oars and sails. Many model boats have been found in Egyptian tombs. They were put there to provide the dead person with transportation in the next world. Archaeologists have also found a number of actual boats, including one built about 4,500 years ago for King Khufu. The **dismantled** ship was buried in a pit next to the Great Pyramid at Giza. Experts **reconstructed** it to form a royal barge over 130 feet (40 m) long.

Model boats were often placed in tombs to help dead souls travel to the next world.

Glossary

bartering trading one item for another
debens copper weight
dismantled taken apart into pieces
ebony a very valuable type of wood

reconstructed rebuilt or put together again
transportation the ways of traveling from place to place

CASE STUDY

Donkeys were used to transport harvested crops.

DONKEYS

The discovery of many donkey skeletons in a cemetery in Maadi and some wall artwork confirm that donkeys were the main way that Egyptians traveled on land. These animals were used for long trading and mining expeditions, too. But donkeys cannot survive for long without food and water. Travelers needed to take plenty of supplies with them, especially when they crossed the hot desert. All peasants kept donkeys because farming would have been almost impossible to manage without them. Sometimes, donkeys were also used to transport the harvested corn to the threshing floor. Horses were not introduced in Egypt until about 1650 B.C.

See also: The Land of Egypt 4–5, Pyramids and Tombs 14–15, Farming 18–19, At Home 26–27

War and Weapons

Although the ancient Egyptians were not particularly warlike people, they were quick to fight their enemies in order to expand their empire. Later pharaohs often led **military campaigns** themselves. Before any campaign, the Egyptians called upon the gods to protect the army and help them defeat their enemies. Scribes accompanied the army into battle and kept a daily record of the war.

THE ARMY

It is estimated that, at its height, the Egyptian army was made up of about one hundred thousand men. The army was huge but well organized and highly disciplined. A strict line of command led from the pharaoh down through the generals and officers of different ranks who commanded the units. The army was split into divisions of five thousand men each (four thousand foot-soldiers and one thousand **charioteers**). The divisions were named after Egyptian gods, such as Amun, Ptah, and Ra. The army's long chain of command is clear from this letter:

*Come, [let me tell] you the woes of the soldier, and how many are his superiors: the general, the troop-commander, the officer who leads, the standard-bearer, the lieutenant, the scribe, the commander of fifty, and the garrison-captain.**

Some men in the army were professional soldiers, but others were forced to join for major campaigns.

War scenes, like the one on this chest, were often painted to record the events that took place on the battlefield.

*Source: Instructions of the scribe Nebmare-nakht for his pupil Wenemdiamun Miriam Lichtheim, Late New Kingdom

Word Discovery

archer *person who uses a bow and arrows*
combat *fighting between*
individuals or groups
conquer *win by force*
hierarchy *line of command*
infantry *soldiers who fought on foot*

WEAPONS

The daggers that were used in battle would have been similar to these, which were found in Tutankhamun's tomb.

Many weapons have been excavated from tombs. The weapons show that Egyptian soldiers fought with spears, battle-axes, bows and arrows, and daggers made of wood and bronze. For protection, soldiers carried wooden and leather shields and wore light armor made of leather and bronze. During the New Kingdom, the horse and **chariot** were introduced and had a big impact on Egyptian warfare.

Egyptian chariots were pulled by two horses and were just big enough for two soldiers to stand in. One soldier drove the chariot while the other attacked the enemy with a bow and arrows or a spear. Chariots have only been found in the tombs of pharaohs and the rich because even charioteers had to buy their own chariots.

Glossary

campaigns the preparation for battles and the battles themselves
chariot an open, two-wheeled battle vehicle pulled by horses
charioteers people who drive a chariot
military relating to soldiers, weapons, or war
rebel going against authority
siege when a town and its people are surrounded by an enemy
surrendered gave in to let the other side win

See also: Pharaohs 6–7, Language and Writing 8–9, Religion 10–11, Work and Play 20–21

CASE STUDY

Pharaoh Tuthmosis III is remembered as Egypt's greatest warrior-king.

The Battle of Megiddo

In 1457 B.C., Pharaoh Tuthmosis III led the Egyptian army against the **rebel** forces of the Prince of Kadesh. Tuthmosis gathered an army of ten thousand men and stormed the city of Megiddo, which finally **surrendered** after a grueling **siege**. A scribe recorded the entire event, and his battle report was carved on the walls of the Temple of Karnak in Thebes:

*All the princes of all the northern countries are cooped up within it. The capture of Megiddo is the capture of a thousand towns.**

Tuthmosis' 17 victorious military campaigns earned him the title of Egypt's greatest warrior-king.

*Source: Inscription from the Amen Temple at Karnak, c. 1460 B.C.

At Home

How well ancient Egyptians lived depended upon whether they were rich or poor. The wealthy enjoyed luxurious lifestyles, but life was much harder for people who were poor. More details are known about the lives of rich Egyptians than the lives of others, because the rich left many more objects and buildings behind.

HOUSES

Archaeological remains show that ancient Egyptian houses were made of brick. The bricks were made from mud taken from the Nile River.

Wall paintings indicate that houses were painted white. Windows were small and high to help block out the heat and keep the houses cool.

Poor Egyptians may have lived in houses like this terracotta model that dates from about 1900 B.C.

Wealthy Egyptians lived in large, spacious houses. Paintings show that some homes had shady gardens and pools, too. Inside, the houses were **opulently** decorated with paintings on the walls and tiles on the floors. Poor Egyptians had much smaller homes, often with only one room for the whole family. These houses were simply decorated with little furniture. If the land and property were shared among a number of people, a list of rights was drawn up to prevent conflicts. These rights may have been similar to the list below:

You may go up [to] and down [from] the roof on the stairway of this aforesaid house and you may go in and out [of the front hallway by means of the] main doorway ... and [you] may make any alteration on it ... in proportion to your aforesaid one-eighteenth share ...*

*Source: A bill of sale dating from the middle of the third century B.C.

FOOD AND DRINK

*Wealthy Egyptians frequently held **banquets** at which many courses of meat, poultry, and fruit were served.*

Ancient Egyptians ate a variety of foods, including fruit, vegetables, meat, fish, ducks, and geese. Poorer people had simple diets, probably consisting of bread, beans, onions, and vegetables, with less meat and more fish. Archaeologists have mainly relied on wall paintings to determine the Egyptian diet, but a few recipes written on **ostraca** have also survived. Beer was a popular drink with Egyptians. To **brew** beer, loaves of bread were broken into pieces and mixed with water. The beer was left to **ferment** and then was strained to get rid of any lumps. A temple inscription hints at beer's popularity in ancient times:

*The mouth of a perfectly contented man is filled with beer.**

*Source: Temple Inscription, 2200 B.C.

At Home Glossary

banquets feasts
brew to soak ingredients in water to make beer, coffee, or tea
ferment to turn into alcohol
opulently done with a lot of money

ostraca broken piece of pottery or a flake of limestone with writing on it
throwstick a wooden stick, like a boomerang, used for killing birds
water birds birds that live near water, such as ducks or swans

CASE STUDY

Hunting and Fishing

In addition to growing their own food, Egyptians also went hunting and fishing. Many tomb paintings show them catching birds and animals and fish on the Nile River. Fish were caught with hooks and lines, with nets slung between two boats, or in traps. Larger fish were caught with spears. **Water birds** were killed by hurling a wooden **throwstick** at them. Wealthy Egyptians also enjoyed hunting desert animals for sport. These animals included antelopes, hares, and foxes. Even kings enjoyed hunting, revealed by accounts such as this one from Pharaoh Amenhotep that describes a bull-hunting expedition:

*There are wild bulls in the desert, in the region of Sheta. His Majesty set out during the night downstream in the royal boat ... [killing] a total of 96 wild bulls.**

Fishing and hunting were necessary for food but also enjoyed as sport.

See also: Farming 18–19, Work and Play 20–21, Trade and Transportation 22–23, At Home 26–27

*Source: Amenhotep III, c. 1415 B.C.

Families

Family life was very important to the ancient Egyptians. Children were **cherished** and adults adopted children if they were unable to have any of their own. The father was the head of the family, but women had many rights and privileges that were unusual in the ancient world. Both sons and daughters could **inherit** their parents' money and property. Old people were well looked after and usually lived with their families, who greatly respected them.

SICKNESS AND HEALTH

Egyptian doctors were highly skilled and well regarded. They may have trained at medical schools that were attached to temples.

The best doctors worked in the royal court. Others worked in the community or for the army. By studying dead animal bodies, doctors had a good idea of how the human body worked and how to treat diseases. Some of the treatments listed in ancient **texts**, however, seem unlikely to been successful:

Diagnosis: One having a wound above his eyebrow. An ailment which I will treat.

Treatment: Now after thou hast stitched it, thou shouldst bind fresh meat upon it the first day. If thou findest that the stitching of this wound is loose, thou shouldst ... treat it with grease and honey every day until he recovers.*

Religion was also used in healing. Doctors recited spells and prayers over their patients. Some patients spent a night in the temple, hoping for a miracle cure.

This temple carving shows a selection of medical instruments used by doctors.

*Source: The Edwin Smith medical papyrus, probably Old Kingdom in origin

Word Discovery

compose *put together words, music, or thoughts*
contract *a written agreement*
discipline *punishment*
education *process of learning*
legal *having to do with the law*
matrimony *marriage*
symptom *sign of a problem*
union *joining together*

LOVE AND MARRIAGE

Most marriages were arranged by parents who believed they could identify the best match for their children. Girls from poor families might marry as early as 12 years old. Scribes advised men to treat their wives properly:

*If you take a wife ... she will be attached to you doubly, if her chain is pleasant ... If you are wise, love your wife ... Fill her stomach, clothe her back ... Be not brutal; **tact** will influence her better than violence.**

A wife could **divorce** her husband if she was badly treated. She was then free to marry again if she wanted. Most marriages lasted a lifetime, however, and many couples were even buried in the same grave. Unlike other civilizations of the time, Egyptian men were not allowed more than one wife at a time.

Marriage and family were very important in Egyptian life.

*Source: Papyrus Lansing, late New Kingdom

CASE STUDY

School

Most Egyptian children did not go to school. Girls helped their mothers at home, while boys learned their father's trade and began to earn a living. But some children went to schools attached to temples or even to the royal court. These schools were for boys only. They learned to read and write by copying and **memorizing** long texts. Later, they might go on to higher education and learn to write legal documents and letters. Most well-educated boys became scribes. If a boy did not listen to his teacher, he might be beaten, as shown in these words of a frustrated teacher to one of his students:

But though I beat you with every kind of stick, you do not listen. If I knew another way of doing it, I would do it for you, that you might listen.*

Only a small number of children went to school. They learned to read and write by copying texts like this one.

Glossary

cherished deeply loved and cared for
divorce the legal ending of a marriage contract
inherit to be given a person's money when that person dies
memorizing learning by heart, committing to one's memory
tact saying or doing something in a way that is not offensive
texts things written down

See also: Language and Writing 8–9, Religion 10–11, Work and Play 20–21, At Home 26–27

*Source: The Precepts of Ptoh-Hotep, 2200 B.C.

Clothes and Jewelry

Ancient Egyptians, both rich and poor, seem to have taken great care with their appearance. Egyptian fashion changed very slowly over hundreds of years, and people did not have lots of new looks and styles to try. Instead, they took pride in keeping themselves and their clothes neat and clean. Both men and women liked to wear makeup and jewelry, and many beautiful pieces of jewelry have been found in Egyptian tombs.

CLOTHES

The many paintings of people that have been found in tombs show the kinds of clothing the ancient Egyptians wore.

Most clothing was light weight and loose fitting to help keep people cool in the hot climate. All clothes were made from **linen**. A man's main **garment** was a practical linen loin cloth or a simple **kilt** that was wrapped around his waist and tied with a knot. Women wore long, tunic-style dresses. Sometimes, they wore cloaks or shawls over their shoulders. People wore simple sandals made from **papyrus** reeds on their feet. It was common, though, for Egyptians to go barefoot and carry their sandals, wearing them when it was necessary.

A middle-class man and woman are dressed in finely pleated white linen clothes in this painting from a tomb at Deir el-Medina.

Word Discovery

amulet *lucky charm*
elaborate *fancy*
fashionable *stylish*

pigments *colorings*
scarab beetle *a type of beetle found in the desert; a sacred*

symbol of the sun god
weaving *way of making cloth*

JEWELRY

Wide collars made of many Roman beads were popular throughout Egyptian history.

Archaeological evidence suggests that all Egyptians of both sexes liked to wear jewelry. Poorer people wore rings, necklaces, and earrings made from less expensive metals, such as copper, decorated with colored stones and glazes. Wealthy Egyptians wore gold and silver that was inlaid with glass or semi-precious stones, such as red carnelian, deep blue lapis lazuli, and light blue turquoise. Egyptian jewelers became experts at working these metals and stones into beautiful necklaces, **pendants**, bracelets, earrings, anklets, and rings. Many pieces of jewelry included sacred symbols that were worn as lucky charms. The tomb of King Tutankhamun contained a magnificent collection of jewelry that revealed the wealth of the pharaohs and the skill of their jewelers.

Glossary

cosmetics makeup, perfumes, and other beauty products
garment a piece of clothing
kilt a short, skirt-like garment
kohl black eyeliner

linen cloth woven from fibers from the flax plant
ochre a type of clay
papyrus type of reed plant used to make many things
pendants types of necklaces

CASE STUDY

Hair and Makeup

Egyptian art shows that most men and women wore their hair cut short. This style would have been more comfortable in Egypt's hot weather. But on special occasions, such as at banquets and official functions, wealthier people liked to wear black wigs made from wool or human hair. Makeup was also widely used. Both men and women lined their eyes with a black paint called **kohl**. They painted their lips and cheeks red with powered red **ochre**. **Cosmetics** were often kept in highly decorated or carved containers. Mirrors were made from polished copper or bronze and not from glass.

Egyptians stored makeup in colorful containers. The containers pictured above were found in various tombs.

See also: Pyramids and Tombs 14–15, Trade and Transportation 22–23, At Home 26–27, Families 28–29

Index

TIME LINE OF ANCIENT EGYPT

About 5000 B.C.
The strip of land by the Nile River becomes known as Lower Egypt (northern part) and Upper Egypt (southern part).

About 3100 B.C.
Lower and Upper Egypt are united under one ruler named Menes.

2686–2181 B.C.
Old Kingdom

2680 B.C.
Egypt's first pyramid is built at Saqqara.

About 2580 B.C.
The building of the Great Pyramid at Giza is completed.

2181–2055 B.C.
First Intermediate Period

2055–1650 B.C.
Middle Kingdom

2055 B.C.
Upper and Lower Egypt are reunited by Mentuhotep II. The first great temples are built at Karnak.

1650–1550 B.C.
Second Intermediate Period
The Hyksos invade from Palestine and nearby and conquer Lower Egypt.

1550–1069 B.C.
New Kingdom

1550 B.C.
The Hyksos are driven out of Egypt.

1504–1492 B.C.
Pharaoh Thutmosis I reigns. He is the first Egyptian ruler to have a rock-cut tomb in the Valley of the Kings.

1352–1336 B.C.
Pharaoh Akhenaten rules Egypt.

1336–1327 B.C.
Tutankhamen is pharaoh.

1279–1213 B.C.
Ramses II (Ramses the Great) rules Egypt. The temple at Abu Simbel is built.

1184–1153 B.C.
Ramses III reigns.

1069–747 B.C,
Third Intermediate Period

747–332 B.C.
Late Period

525–404 B.C.
Persia invades and takes control of Egypt. After the Persians are defeated, the country returns to Egyptian rule.

About 450 B.C.
The Greek traveler and historian Herodotus visits Egypt.

323 B.C.–A.D. 395
Greek-Roman Period

343–332 B.C.
Persia invades again and regains control of Egypt.

332 B.C.
The Persians are overthrown by the armies of Alexander the Great. Egypt becomes part of the Greek Empire.

196 B.C.
The Rosetta Stone is carved.

51–30 B.C.
Cleopatra VII rules. Egypt is conquered by the Romans and becomes part of the Roman Empire.